HOW TO
PICK A
WINE

By Lee M. Cunningham

of

Fore Vintages
Bobcaygeon, Canada
www.forevintages.com

How to Pick a Wine
by Lee M. Cunningham
Second edition 2008

Published by
Lee M. Cunningham
Fore Vintages, Bobcaygeon, Canada

Book design by Louise Gaillard, One Stop Books

ISBN-13   978-0-9816481-0-1
ISBN-10   0-9816481-0-X

HOW TO PICK A
WINE

Have you ever walked into a wine store and felt intimidated by the many choices before you?

This handy, informative guide written by the founder of **Fore Vintages, Lee M. Cunningham,** will make everything about the fermented grape much clearer for the novice and intermediate wine buyer.

Within these pages you will learn about the different types of wine (red, white, rose, champagne, sparkling) available, vintage wines, and even how to pair wine with food for optimal flavor. This guide is the first in a series from Mr. Cunningham.

This guide will put you on the road to becoming a true wine enthusiast!

Dedicated to all those people who have
helped me find my passion in life, and to my
wonderful wife for supporting me in
pursuing that passion.

Table of Contents

Introduction

Introduction

Have you ever stared at the endless rows of wine bottles in a store or at a long list of wines in a restaurant menu and thought to yourself, "How do I pick the right one?"

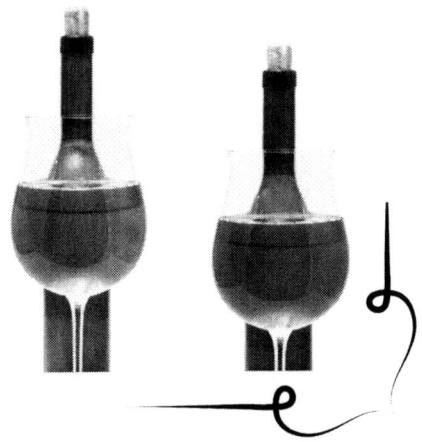

Well, it used to happen to me all the time. The worst part was, when someone would come over and ask me if I needed any help, I would wince. "Of course I needed help," I would think to myself. But I couldn't admit this to this person in front of me because I assumed I would look stupid. And if I tried to pretend to be knowledgeable, I knew I would look even worse.

Does this sound like you? Well congratulations in getting the concept of my book. Those days are over for you.

After all, there are so many wines to choose from. Not

only are there whites and reds to sort through, but different styles of the same wines, as well. Add to this the hundreds, if not thousands, of wineries producing wine, and it's understandable why you may be confused about wine.

Fortunately, you don't have to feel frustrated. Knowledge is power, and this book will give you with the tools to make informed choices - ones that will turn you into a pro in no time.

Like the other books in our "how to" series, I will teach you how to navigate through the plethora of wine choices. I will share with you the differences between whites, blushes, and reds (outside the obvious one of color), the most common type of wines, the best regions to consider when shopping for a bottle, the best vintage years, and which foods go best with a particular wine.

Once you arm yourself with the knowledge I'm about to present, you'll become confident in your wine selections. Eventually you'll learn even more about your favorites.

Time's wasting and there is so much wine out there to enjoy. So let's get started!

Cheers and Enjoy!

Types of Wine

Types of Wine

Types of Wine

Let's start with wine basics. Four main types of wine exist: red, white, rosé, and sparkling wine/champagne. If you've ever shopped for wines, then you know there are also variations on these styles, such as dessert wines, fortified wines, and fruit wines. But let's keep things simple for now and discuss these four types of popular table wines in greater depth.

Red Wine:
Red wine gets its color from the skins of the grapes which are imparted to the juice during fermentation. Along with the skins, the grapes pits and stems is also fermented with the juice. It's similar to how beets impart colour to boiling water. Depending on the ripeness of the grapes and the style of wine being produced, the fermentation process can take up to 2 weeks.

Fermentation is the process of the sugar in the grapes coming into contact with cultured yeast - one that produces predictable results and flavours -- added to the juice. Sugar plus yeast in the presence of juice produces an alcoholic fermentation. This type of fermentation creates alcohol and carbon dioxide. The wine retains the alcohol, while losing the carbon dioxide into the air.

6

A quality red wine, no matter where it is produced around the world, will have a balance of fruitiness, tanginess (acidity), and pleasant bitterness and dryness (tannin and astringency). Quality reds also have consistency in how they smell, taste and finish on the palate. A red wine that falls short is one that may have great flavours, but dissipates off the palate the moment you swallow it. Or a wine that has what is referred to as a "muted" nose. This means the wine has very subtle or non descript aromas.

A great, well-balanced red wine, however, will have a forward nose, a palate that backs up what your nose tells you, lots of interesting flavours and an aftertaste that lingers on your palate long after the wine has vanished. Some of the most common red grape varieties used to produce red wine in the New World wine regions are Cabernet Sauvignon, Merlot, Cabernet Franc, Pinot Noir, Syrah (Shiraz), Gamay, Sangiovese, and Zinfandel. Each of these varieties take on individualistic characteristics depending on the terroir of the region in which the grapes are grown, and even within the vineyard. Terroir is the interplay between geography, climate and soil.

Red wines and some whites contain tannins. Tannins come from the skins, stem, and pips of the grape, from sur-lie aging (aging the wine on its dead yeast cells) and from the oak barrels used to ferment and/or age the wine. Tannin adds complexity and structure, while also contributing to the wine's aging potential in the cellar. Tannin gives wine its characteristic puckery, dry sensation.

Finding red wines you enjoy will depend on your level of appreciation for tannin. Do you like smooth velvety reds with low tannin or big, strong reds with heavy tannin. There is no right answer. Wine is a personal thing.

I'm sure you've heard that red wine should be served at room temperature. Well, this is an old rule that derived from Europe before "electric heat." So, in essence, you really want to serve your reds at "cellar temperature." They are at their best with a bit of a chill.

Red wines are best served at a temperature of 16-18 degrees Celsius or 60-64 degrees Fahrenheit.

Traditionally, you would serve red meats with your red wine. Steak, roasts, venison, duck, pork ribs, and rich stews are typical foods to partner with red wine. However, today there are no real hard rules on what wine you can sip with a particular dish. It's really up to your own personal preferences.

Rosé Wine:
We now move onto rosé, blush or white Zinfandel wines. These wines are made using red grapes, such as Zinfandel or Grenache. In contrast to red wines, rosés are only in contact with the skins during fermentation for a short period of time, creating their characteristic blush hue. They are certainly beautiful to look at. Their colour can range from light pink to deep salmon.

Rosés can range in quality, just like other table wines. They can possess finesse and be quite complex or they can be yummy and easy drinking. However, most roses are vinified for immediate consumption. Because they are generally low in

9

alcohol and tannin, roses are mostly "drinkable now" and so not meant to rest in your wine cellar for years. So have a barbecue for friends and serve your rosés. As a summer time or hot weather wine, a chilled glass of rosé can be very refreshing.

This style of wine is best served at a temperature of 8-10 degrees Celsius or 46-50 degrees Fahrenheit. If you're not one to consider temperatures, then throw the wine in the refrigerator for at least an hour.

White Wine:
The most common grapes used in making white wines in New World wine regions are Sauvignon Blanc, Chardonnay, Semillon, Chenin Blanc, Riesling, Gewürztraminer, and Pinot Blanc.

In contrast to red or rosé winemaking, and in the vinification of whites, the skins, stems, and pips are separated from the juice early on. Once these are removed, the grape juice is processed in much the same manner as all other wines.

Whites can be produced in a variety of styles from crisp and dry to semi-sweet, to fermented and aged in oak or vinified into a dessert wine. Crisp versions are tangy and fruity, while oak-aged ones have more bitterness and dryness (tannin and astringency). High alcohol white wines made in warm climates often have a creamy, buttery texture much like butter.

White wines are best served at a temperature of 8-10 degrees Celsius or 46-50 degrees Fahrenheit. Or, just like with rosés, put your whites in the refrigerator for at least an hour before serving.

**Sparkling Wine /
Champagne:**
Finally the crowd favorite: sparkling wine and champagne. Typically seen at celebrations, sparkling wine is a great beverage to have before a meal as an aperitif. It helps cleanse your palate between bites.

The term "Champagne" is the name of the region where the bubbly is produced, as well as the name of the wine itself.

Only wine produced in this region can be called Champagne. In North America and in the rest of the world, winemakers create sparkling wine using the traditional method called "methode Champenoise." (I'll cover this process further on.)

In order to produce a rosé or pink Champagne there are two methods. The first is to add some red wine during the process. The second method is to leave the skins in contact with the juice for a short period of time.

In bottling the wine, vintners only pick exceptional years to class Champagne as "vintage." For example, in the 1980s only three vintage Champagnes were produced: 1982, 1983, and 1989.

Sparkling wine or Champagne is best served at a temperature of 8-10 degrees Celsius or 46-50 degrees Fahrenheit.

Keep it in an ice bucket chilling after you have opened it.

"Method Champenoise"
To produce Champagne, the French use a vinification process called "methode Champenoise" This basically

means the wine undergoes its secondary fermentation in individual bottles rather than in a large tank. As a result, the bubbles are small and longer lasting, a sign of quality.

Method Champenoise is a labor intense process that allows the wine to ferment and age in its bottle rather than undergoing a process called charmat where it ferments in a pressurized tank and then is bottled.

The following are steps used in the process:

Harvest – The harvest will usually take place in the fall, late September or early October.

Pressing the grapes – The grapes are only allowed to be pressed a maximum of three times. The first pressing will produce high quality juice while the last two pressings will produce juice used in the making ofinexpensive Champagnes.

Fermentation – The juice undergoes its first fermentation, taking between 2 to 3 weeks.

Blending – This is the most important step in the process. Some of the winemaker's key decisions are what grapes to blend, what years to blend, and what percentage of each variety to use.

Liqueur de Tirage – The wine is then placed in its permanent bottle. The winemaker then adds a blend of sugar and yeast known as "Liquer de Tirage." This begins the wine's secondary fermentation.

Second Fermentation – During secondary fermentation, carbon dioxide is produced, giving the wine its effervesce.

Aging – This is a key point in determining the quality of Champagne.

Riddling – As a wine undergoes fermentation, the dead yeast cells fall to the bottom of the bottle. In order to remove the sediment before going to market, the bottles must be riddled or slowly turned with the neck increasingly tipped downward. Riddling takes approximately 6 to 8 weeks because the bottle is turned very slowly. Once completed, the bottle is fully upside down, allowing all the sediment to settle in the neck.

Degorgement – This is the fun part of the making of Champagne. The neck of the bottle is immersed into a brine solution, which freezes the sediment. Once the sediment is frozen, the cap is taken off the bottle. The sediment pops out because of the force of the pressure from the carbon dioxide that has built up in the bottle.

Dosage – A combination of wine and sugar are then added to the Champagne. The amount added depends on its level of dryness or sweetness.

On the label of Champagne and sparkling wines, the following terms are used to indicate the level of dosage (sweetness.) Dosage is expressed as a percentage of the volume of wine in the bottle.

Without dosage, the wines can be called Brut Zero, Brut de Brut, Ultra Brut, Brut Sauvage, Brut Total, Brut Nature.

Brut - up to 1% (bone dry)
Extra Sec (extra dry) from 1% to 3%
Sec (dry) - from 3% to 5%
Demi-Sec (semisweet) - from 5% to 8%
Doux (sweet) - from 8% to 15%

Recorking – The final cork is placed in the bottle. Both the bottle and the cork are stouter than their wine counterparts because the contents are pressurized.

Getting Started

Getting Started

As you go through the ensuing pages, please note that the key regions, best years, and food/wine pairings are generalizations. There are always exceptions to the rules.

If relatively new to wine, you've probably heard the old axiom, "white with chicken and fish and red with red meats." This rule is fast becoming obsolete. More and more people are finding interesting and rewarding wine and food pairings that break these rules.

It's okay if you choose to stay the course with this philosophy. But as you gain experience and taste more wines, you'll no doubt find yourself wanting to experiment with various ingredients, dishes, and wine combinations.

Tips for Buying Wine:
- If you want a wine to go with delicate fish, like sole, choose low alcohol whites from cool climates.
- If you want a wine to partner with fatty fish like salmon and tuna, go for whites with higher alcohol from warm climates. Fatty fish also work with light, fruity reds, like Pinot Noir.
- When choosing wine to complement food, consider the sauces and spices first. Then think about the weight of the dish and find a wine with matching weight.
- Red and white wines with some sweetness always work with a whole range of cheeses. Their sweetness complements the saltiness in cheese, like the flavour sensation of eating popcorn and chocolate at the movies.
- If you're unsure as to what wines work with specific dishes, stick to regional pairings like Italian wine and Italian food or French wine with the cuisine of France
- If you want a wine to complement game meats or beef, hunt for a red from a warm climate with high alcohol.

- If you enjoy white wines that are not too tangy or two bitter, then buy ones with low alcohol (about 12 percent), such as pinot blanc, vidal and un-oaked chardonnay.
- If you like red wines that are not too tangy or two bitter then buy ones with low alcohol (about 12 to 13 percent) such as merlot and shiraz.
- For large gatherings (weddings, showers, office parties, holiday affairs) the aim is to please most of the guests - of all ages -- most of the time. So, buy wines that are not too tangy or too bitter, such as pinot blanc, vidal, unoaked chardonnay, merlot and shiraz.
- If you enjoy the more delicate wines with finesse but with layers of flavours, purchase ones from cooler climates. Cooler climatic regions are Ontario, Oregan, Burguny, Bordeaux, etc.
- If you enjoy heavier wines with big, forward fruit flavours, purchase ones from warmer climates, such as South Africa, Chile, Australia.
- If you like red wines with more earthy character, stick to those produced in France, Italy and Spain.

Red Wine

Red Wine

The following is an overview of the major red wines along with their characteristics, best regions and years and food matches:

Cabernet Sauvignon (Cah-burr-NAY Sow-vee-NYOH)

Description:

- Cabernets can be mellow and mild or hearty and rich. It has a deep red color with the primary taste being black currant. Other overtones can include blackberry and mint. Traditionally aged in oak, the wine also takes on an oaky, vanilla flavor. Higher quality cabs age extremely well (although a bit slowly), developing a sprinkling of five or six tastes within it over time.

Best Regions to Buy and Key Years:

- California – 1995, 1996, 1997, 1999, 2001, 2002, 2003, 2004
- Australia – 1994, 1996, 1997, 1998, 1999, 2001, 2002, 2003, 2004
- Chile – 1993, 1995, 1996, 1997, 1998, 1999, 2000
- South Africa – 1996, 1997,

(continued)

21

1998, 1999, 2000, 2001
- Argentina – 1994, 1996, 1997, 1998, 1999, 2000, 2001
- Canada – 1993, 1994, 1995, 1997, 1998, 1999, 2000, 2002, 2005, 2007

Food Matches:
- Rich meats, roast beef, veal, venison, duck, lamb, strong cheeses, vegetable stews, and tomato based sauces.

Pinot Noir (pee-noh NWAHR)
Description:
- Soft, slightly fruity, fresh, earthy aroma. It is easy to drink and has a range of colors, from cherry red to purple red and even brown as the wine ages. The wine offers a pleasant, mild taste with a refreshing level of tanginess (acidity). This grape in a glass will sometimes reveal different layers of flavors, including earth, leather, vanilla, and cherry. When present the fruity flavors of jam often taste like raspberry, strawberry, and plum.

Best Regions to Buy and Key Years:
- France – 1993, 1995, 1996, 1997, 1998, 1999, 2002, 2003

(continued)

- California – 1997, 1998, 1999, 2000, 2001, 2002, 2003, 2004, 2005
- South Africa – 1996, 1997, 1998, 1999, 2000, 2001
- New Zealand – 1998, 1999, 2000, 2002, 2003
- Canada – 1998, 1999, 2000, 2002, 2005, 2007

Food Matches:
- Grilled steak, lamb, stews, mildly seasoned pastas, cedar plank salmon, lasagna, and mild to strong cheeses.

Merlot (Mehr-LOW)
Description:
- While Merlots are quite often less tannic (astringent) and more lush than Cabernets, they are still medium to full-bodied. Merlots are usually deep in color and can have a fairly high alcohol content. Wines from this variety can also have flavors reminiscent of cherry, plum, and even chocolate in the taste. Their aromas can be fruity and herbal.

Best Regions to Buy and Key Years:
- California – 1994, 1995, 1996, 1997, 1999, 2001, 2002, 2003, 2004
- Australia – 1996, 1997, 1998, 1999, 2001, 2002, 2003, 2004

(continued)

- Chile – 1993, 1995, 1996, 1997, 1998, 1999, 2000
- South Africa – 1994, 1995, 1997, 1998, 1999, 2000, 2001
- Argentina – 1997, 1198, 1999, 2000, 2001, 2002
- Canada – 1998, 1999, 2000, 2002, 2005, 2007

Food Matches:
- Rich meats, roast beef, veal, venison, duck, strong cheeses, vegetable stews, and tomato based sauces.

Syrah (Shiraz) (See-RAH)
Description:
- Syrah and Shiraz are the same grape. Australia, South Africa, and some other New World locations use the term "Shiraz," whereas the Old World regions, such as France, use the term "Syrah." Despite its name, this is the same grape. It's character depends on where it is  grown and vinified. Syrah's aromas and flavours are pepper, blackberry, herbs, and cinnamon. Often there are additional notes of licorice, bitter chocolate, and mocha. Shiraz can be downright fruity with ripe berry character

(continued)

and velvety texture. This wine pairs well with spicy food.

Best Regions to Buy and Key Years:
- France – 1995, 1996, 1998, 1999, 2000, 2001, 2003, 2004
- California – 1997, 1999, 2001, 2002, 2003, 2004
- Australia – 1997, 1998, 1999, 2000, 2001, 2002, 2003, 2004, 2005
- South Africa – 1997, 1998, 1999, 2000, 2001

Food Matches:
- Grilled steak, lamb, stews, spicy pastas, pizza, and Mexican and Cajun dishes.

Cabernet Franc (Cah-burr-NAY Frahnk)

Description:
- Cabernet Franc has a deep ruby color with a hint of garnet. It is lighter in color and tannins than Cabernet Sauvignon. This wine is typically somewhat berry-like and spicy in aroma. Instead of being used as a standalone varietal, Cabernet Franc is sometimes used as a secondary element in blended red wines, such as Bordeaux or Meritage. However, some wineries are beginning to market Cabernet Franc as a separate product. Cabernet Franc grows very

(continued)

well in cool climates like Ontario, producing outstanding varietal wine.

Best Regions to Buy and Key Years:
- Australia – 1994, 1996, 1997, 1998, 1999, 2001, 2002, 2003, 2004
- New Zealand – 1994, 1995, 1997, 1998, 1999, 2000, 2002, 2003
- California – 1995, 1996, 1997, 1999, 2001, 2002, 2003, 2004
- Canada – 1993, 1994, 1995, 1997, 1998, 1999, 2000, 2002, 2005, 2007

Food Matches:
- This wine can stand can stand up to rich and robust fare, cooked or grilled red meat, game, and chicken, most cheeses and cold cuts, pizza, and barbecued meats.

Bordeaux (Bor-dough)
Description:
- Almost all of the wines in Bordeaux are made from blends. The major grapes are Cabernet Sauvignon, Merlot, and Cabernet Franc. A medium to full bodied wine, Bordeaux ages well but can be enjoyed near term as well. Bordeaux has finesse with medium, well struc-

(continued)

tured tannins. There are five key regions in Bordeaux. When looking for a Bordeaux the year is more important than its price. Buy the year with the price you can afford from one of the regions I list. I have listed the key years below.

Best Regions to Buy and Key Years:
- Medoc, Pomerol, Graves, St-Emilion, Sauternes – 1988, 1989, 1990, 1995, 1996, 1998, 2000, 2001, 2002, 2003, 2004, 2005

Food Matches:
- Grilled steak, lamb, roast duck, herbed pastas, veal, and Camembert, Brie, or Roquefort cheeses.

Chateauneuf du Pape (Shot-toe-noof duh Pop)

Description:
- Châteauneuf-du-Pape permits thirteen different varieties of grapes to be blended together. Grenache is usually the predominant grape. Others include Cinsault, Counoise, Mourvedre, Muscardin, Syrah, Terret Noir, and Vaccarèse. White grapes include Grenache Blanc, Bourboulenc, Clairette, Picardin, Roussanne,

(continued)

27

and Picpoul. Although generally considered full-bodied and powerful wines, red Chateauneuf du Pape is usually lower in tannin than Syrah. Chateauneuf du Pape is high in alcohol; between 14% and 16%. It offers plenty of ripe plumy fruit flavors with layers of spice and softly integrated tannins. A nice medium red wine.

Best Regions to Buy and Key Years:
- Southern Rhone Valley, France – 1988, 1989, 1990, 1995, 1997, 1998, 1999, 2000, 2001, 2003, 2004

Food Matches:
- Grilled steaks, beef stews, game stews or roasts, venison, hard cheeses, aged cheddar and soft cheeses.

Zinfandel (Zin-fan-DELL)
Description:
- Zinfandel is deep red, bordering on black. It is a spicy, peppery wine, with lots of forward, big, berry fruit flavour. California produces a whole range of outstanding Zinfandel wines. With its peppery notes Zinfandel pairs well with BBQ foods.

(continued)

Best Regions to Buy and Key Years:

- California – 1993, 1994, 1996, 2001, 2002, 2003, 2004

Food Matches:

- Grilled steak, pastas, pizza, grilled beef burgers, baby back ribs, sausages, and chicken.

Meritage (Meh-rih-TIJ)

Description:

- Meritage is the term created to describe North American wines made from blending traditional Bordeaux grape varieties. It means "vintages of merit." It is made from two or more of the following grape varieties: Cabernet Sauvignon, Merlot, Cabernet Franc, Malbec, Petite Verdot, St Macaire, Gros Verdot, and Carmenere. Each wine maker will have their percentage of each variety they use to produce their vintage based on their preferences. A medium to full bodied wine, Meritage ages well but can also be enjoyed right away. Meritage is a pleasing red wine with medium tannins.

(continued)

Best Regions to Buy and Key Years:
- California – 1994, 1995, 1996, 1997, 1999, 2001, 2002, 2003, 2004
- Canada – 1993, 1994, 1995, 1997, 1998, 1999, 2000, 2002, 2005, 2007

Food Matches:
- Excellent with beef, lamb, grilled veal, game such as pheasant and poultry.

Gamay Noir (Gah-MAY No-ARE)
Description:
- This ruby red wine offers reflections of violets. Easy to drink, it is usually light to medium bodied, depending on whether it is produced in a cool climate or warm climate. It offers a good backbone of refreshing acidity and has wonderful fruity aromas and flavours. The aroma is of red fruits, namely cherry and plum. It is well balanced with the presence of tannin.

Best Regions to Buy and Key Years:
- France – 1989, 1999, 2000, 2003, 2005
- California – 1994, 1997, 1998, 1999, 2001, 2002, 2003, 2004, 2005
- Canada – 1993, 1994, 1995, 1997, 1998, 1999, 2000, 2002, 2005, 2007

(continued)

Food Matches:
- Grilled Steak, lamb, stews, mildly seasoned pastas, cedar plank salmon, lasagna, and mild to strong cheeses.

Beaujolais (Boe-zho-lay)

Description:
- Most Beaujolais Nouveau are made entirely from the Gamay grape. The wine is fruit forward and light. Unlike most red wines, this particular one undergoes a process called carbonic maceration. The whole grapes are vinified in a carbon dioxide rich environment inside a closed stainless steel tank. As a result the wine is light and fruity and ready to drink immediately. However, this style of wine lacks the complexity and structure of other reds. Beaujolais has similar tastes to other Gamay wines, being light and fruity.

Best Regions to Buy and Key Years:
- France – 1989, 1999, 2000, 2003, 2005

Food Matches:
- Barbequed salmon, spicy sausage, beef stir fry, roast beef, turkey, chicken, and pasta with cream sauce.

(continued)

Chianti (Ki-AHN-tee)

Description:

- Chianti is one of the best-known Italian wines in the world. It is produced primarily from Sangiovese grapes, often with a little Cabernet Franc, Merlot, or Cabernet Sauvignon blended in. Chianti is subtle and less harsh than a Cabernet Sauvignon and more elegant than a Zinfandel or a Syrah. It has high acidity and hints of plum and wild cherry. Its acidity makes Chianti an excellent food partner for spaghetti in tomato sauce. Tomatoes are tangy, thus complementing the same taste sensation in the wine.

Best Regions to Buy and Key Years:

- Italy – 1990, 1997, 1999, 2001, 2004, 2005

Food Matches:

- Grilled steak, grilled meats, lamb, stews, pastas, mild to strong cheeses, and pizza.

Valpolicella (Vahl-poe-lee-CHELL-ah)

Description:

- Usually made by blending three grape varietals: Corvina Veronese, Rondinella, and Molinara. Most Valpolicellas are fruity, medi-

(continued)

um weight reds that serve as good table wines.

Best Regions to buy and key years:
- Italy, Veneto region – 1990, 1993, 1997, 1998, 2000, 2003, 2004, 2005

Food Matches:
- Veal, pork, tomato-based sauces, roasts of meat, and mild to strong cheeses.

Ripasso (Ree-PAH-soe)

Description:
- Ripasso is an Italian term meaning repassed. It is a technique that adds additional flavor and alcohol to the Valpolicella. The unpressed grape skins are used to make a "raisinated" wine called Amarone that is then added to the already blended and fermented Valpolicella. This adds an incredible amount of body, character, and style to an otherwise straightforward wine. The benefits of this process include oxidized and botrytis flavors and additional tannins. The tannins give this wine a few extra years in the cellar as well. The conditions for creating a Ripasso wine only occur in exceptional vintage years.

(continued)

Best Regions to Buy and Key Years:
- Italy, Veneto region – 1990, 1993, 1997, 1998, 2000, 2003, 2004, 2005

Food Matches:
- Grilled steak, grilled or roasted meats, lamb, stews, and mild to strong cheeses.

Amarone (Ah-ma-ROE-nay)

Description:
- Predominantly Corvina grapes are air-dried for three to four months, causing them to shrivel and further concentrate their flavors. Up to a third of their mass (mostly water) is lost during this process, causing the resulting wine to have a high (15-16%) alcohol content. Amarones are aged for five years or more before bottling. Some, but not all, are aged in oak barrels. Amarone (the name means big, bitter one) is lush and complex. It has a powerful, concentrated, almost Port-like texture with hints of mocha.

Best Regions to Buy and Key Years:
- Italy, Veneto region – 1990, 1997, 1998, 1999, 2001, 2003, 2004, 2005

(continued)

Food Matches:

- Rich meats, roast beef, veal, venison, duck, strong cheeses, vegetable stews, and tomato based sauces.

Barolo (Ba-ROE-loe)

Description:

- Big, powerful, and full-bodied with a complex mixture of tastes and textures – wild strawberry, tobacco, chocolate, and vanilla – Barolo gets better and better with age. Barolo is austere and tannic in its youth and requires many years (three years minimum by law) of aging to soften it.

Best Regions to Buy and Key Years:

- Italy, Piedmont region – 1996, 1997, 1998, 1999, 2000, 2001, 2003, 2004, 2005

Food Matches:

- Grilled steak, rich meats, lamb, stews, rich pastas, risottos, and mild to strong cheeses.

White Wine

White Wine

Chardonnay (Shar-doe-nay)

Description:

- This wine possesses rich citrus and fruit flavors, including apple, tangerine, lemon, lime, melon, and oak. More velvety than most whites. If it has been fermented and/or aged in oak then it can also have a creamy, buttery tone to it. Wine drinkers love Chardonnay because of the wide variety of flavors it can possess.

Best Regions to Buy and Key Years:

- France (Burgundy) – 1995, 1996, 1997, 1999, 2002, 2005
- California – 1995, 1997, 1998, 1999, 2001, 2002, 2003, 2004, 2005
- Australia – 1996, 1998, 2001, 2002, 2003, 2004, 2005
- New Zealand – 1996, 1998, 1999, 2003, 2004, 2005
- Canada – 1993, 1995, 1997, 1998, 1999, 2000, 2001, 2002. 2005, 2007

Food Matches:

- A good choice for fish and chicken dishes, pork, and pasta.

Riesling (REES-ling)

Description:

- Rieslings vary in flavor depending on the region in which they are grown, the vineyards in which they are located, and the processes used by each winery. However, sweet Rieslings typically taste of pitted and tropical fruits, such as apricots and peaches, while dry versions can have nuances of citrus fruits like lemon, lime, and grapefruit. Both sweet and dry versions can also have subtle herbal and floral notes as well.

Best Regions to Buy and Key Years:

- Germany – 1996, 1998, 2001, 2002, 2003, 2004, 2005
- France – 1994, 1995, 1998, 2000, 2001
- Australia – 1996, 1998, 2001, 2002, 2003, 2004, 2005
- Canada – 1993, 1995, 1997, 1998, 1999, 2000, 2001, 2002, 2005, 2007

Food Matches:

- Chicken, fish, pastas, pork, Thai or Chinese food, desserts, and cheeses.

Sauvignon Blanc (SOH-veen-yown, blahnk)

Description:

- Sauvignon Blanc and Fumé Blanc both have a distinctively sharp herbal, almost grassy aromas. As with most wines, their flavors vary depending on a number of different factors but their dominating flavors range from green apples, pears, and gooseberries to tropical fruits such as melons and mangos.

Best Regions to Buy and Key Years:

- France – 1997, 2001, 2003, 2005
- Australia – 1998, 1999, 2001, 2002, 2003, 2005
- New Zealand – 1995, 1997, 1998, 1999, 2000, 2001, 2002
- Canada – 1993, 1995, 1997, 1998, 1999, 2000, 2001, 2002, 2005, 2007

(continued)

Food Matches:
- Brie, Gouda, Swiss, and strong cheeses, chicken, poultry, Thai dishes, pastas, pizza, ham, and seafood.

Chablis (Shah-blee)
Description:
- Chablis is made from the Chardonnay grape. Chablis is grown in a very chalky and fossil-rich soil. The soil profile contributes to the wine's character, if not subtly. Four appellations in Chablis are based on the type of land the vines are grown on. They are Chablis, Petit Chablis, Chablis Premier Cru, and Chablis Grand Cru. Chablis is light, crisp, fruity, and floral and is considered a fun, quaffing wine. Chablis produces wines from the majority of the region's vineyards. They are also crisp and refreshing with an elegant aroma. Chablis Premier Cru wines come from specific vineyards that are, in some cases, as good as Grand Cru, but mostly not as concentrated in character. Chablis Grand Cru wines come from seven specific vineyards located on the chalky southwestern slopes of a hill just outside the town of Chablis. These gems are first rate with deep colour, complex flavours and

(continued)

have a greenish tinge.

Best Regions to Buy and Key Years:
- North Burgundy – 1995, 1996, 1999, 2000, 2001, 2002, 2005

Food Matches:
- Seafood, including grilled fish, oysters, and lobster, mild cheeses, and white meats such as chicken, poultry or pork.

Pinot Blanc (Pee-noe BlahN)
Description:
- Pinot Blanc wines are usually dry and high in acidity with flavors of apples and spice. They typically have a very light, neutral aroma. Golden yellow in color, this wine has very smooth overtones. Best enjoyed young.

Best Regions to Buy and Key Years:
- France – 1994, 1995, 1998, 2000, 2001
- Germany – 1996, 1998, 2001, 2002, 2003, 2004, 2005
- California – 1995, 1997, 1998, 1999, 2001, 2002, 2003, 2004, 2005
- Canada – 1993, 1995, 1997, 1998, 1999, 2000, 2001, 2002, 2005, 2007

(continued)

Food Matches:
- Chicken, poultry, Asian and Thai food, sashimi, pasta, clams, mussels, oysters, and fish.

Gewürztraminer (geh-verts-tram-in-er)
Description:
- An aromatic white variety that performs best in cooler climates. Known for its pungent floral aroma and zesty, fruity flavor. Gewürztraminers range from dry and crisp to sweet dessert types. It is not uncommon to notice some *spritz* (fine bubbles on the inside of the glass).

Best Regions to Buy and Key Years:
- Germany – 1996, 1998, 2001, 2002, 2003, 2004, 2005
- France – 1994, 1995, 1998, 2000, 2001
- Canada – 1993, 1995, 1997, 1998, 1999, 2000, 2001, 2002, 2005, 2007

Food Matches:
- Brie, Gouda, herb or pepper crusted cheese, chicken, poultry, turkey, veal, Tex Mex dishes, Tandoori, Chinese and Thai dishes, pastas, lobster, salmon, shrimp, and fruit desserts.

Pinot Gris or Pinot Grigio (pee-noh GREES)(pee-noh GREE-joe)

Description:
- Is a crisp, light, dry wine known for its tangy flavor. Golden yellow in color with aromatic fruity flavors that improve after a couple of years of aging, this wine has very smooth overtones.

Best Regions to Buy and Key Years:
- Italy – 1997, 1998, 1999, 2000, 2003, 2005
- France – 1994, 1995, 1998, 2000, 2003
- Canada – 1993, 1995, 1997, 1998, 1999, 2000, 2001, 2002, 2005, 2007
- Oregon – 1998, 1999, 2000, 2001, 2002,
- California - 1995, 1997, 1998, 1999, 2001, 2002, 2003, 2004, 2005
- New Zealand - 1995, 1997, 1998, 1999, 2000, 2001, 2002
- Australia - 1998, 1999, 2001, 2002, 2003, 2005

Food Matches:
- Seafood, chicken, pizza, Tex Mex dishes, Chinese and Thai dishes, pasta, veal, and cheese.

Rosé

R
o
s
é

Rosé

White Zinfandel

Description:

- An off-dry to sweet, pink-colored Rosé wine that is soft and low in alcohol. White Zinfandel is made from the Zinfandel wine grape which would otherwise produce a bold and spicy red wine.

Key Years:

- White Zinfandel is typically manufactured for immediate consumption rather than for aging.

Best Regions to Buy:

- California

Food Matches:

- Lamb, poultry, chicken, seafood, and mild cheeses.

Rosé

Description:

- Typically made form Rhone style grapes like Syrah. Typically a bigger wine than a White Zinfandel. A fruity wine, it is better served chilled.

Key Years:
- Rosé wines are made to be consumed after bottling with no aging required.

Best Regions to Buy:
- France
- United States
- Spain
- Canada

Food Matches:
- Lamb, poultry, chicken, seafood, and mild cheeses.

Champagne

Champagne

Description:
- Champagne is more than a drink. It is actually a region in France and this region is the only place in the world that can produce a wine that is actually called Champagne. Similar wines from other areas are known as Sparkling Wines (see next section). Most Champagnes are made from a blend of Chardonnay and Pinot Noir. Most Champagne is non-vintage, produced from a blend of years. Medium body with lots of bubbles and very clean taste. Great for starting of a meal or enjoying on a special occasion.

Best Regions to Buy and Key Years:
- Champagne, France – 1985, 1989, 1990, 1995, 1996, 2000, 2002

Food Matches:
- Cheeses, chicken, sushi, pasta, seafood, fruit, and of course, chocolate covered strawberries.

Sparkling Wine

Sparkling Wine

Description:
- This is a wine similar to Champagne, however, it is not usually made using the "Methode Champenoise." Its characteristics are very similar to true Champagne. Since there are many producers all over the world, you will find some very unique styles of Sparkling Wine, including blushes and reds.

Key Years:
- Sparkling Wines are typically made from blends and are not aged. They are produced to be consumed after they are bottled.

Best Regions to Buy:
- France
- California
- Canada
- Spain
- Italy

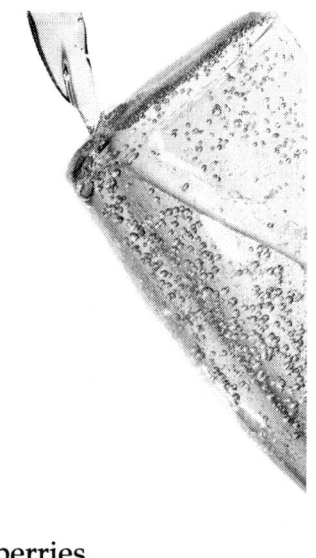

Food Matches:
- Cheeses, chicken, sushi, pasta, seafood, and fruit, especially chocolate covered strawberries.

Enjoy Wine to the Fullest

By now, you should have a solid grounding in the art of selecting the correct wine. You now know the differences between the many varieties on the market, the best vintages, and the best regions for each vintage year.

As a result, you'll never have to fear the wine store aisles or restaurant wine lists again. You can select or order in complete confidence, knowing that you've made a good selection.

But the journey is just beginning. Now that you know the different types of wines, you can begin your search for the ones you like the best. Each winemaker treats their grapes differently and uses different processes, many of which begin in the vineyards where the grapes are grown. As such, no two wines—even two Rieslings or

Merlots from the same year—taste the same. Each has its own unique nuances, flavors, and finishes.

Experimentation is the only way to find your favorites. This not only holds true for the wine itself, but the way you enjoy the process of drinking wine. The choice of glass, the way you store the bottle, and the way you open and pour it all affect the flavors of the wine.

Many of the rituals of wine tasting and enjoyment are based on solid science while others are mixed with myth. We recommend picking up a copy of our other "how to" book, **How to Enjoy Wine**. It is packed with information about how to store your wine, types of glassware, proper tasting techniques, wine openers, and much more. It is a great companion piece to this book and you'll quickly find them both to be essential reference guides as you explore the wonderful world of wine.

Enjoy your journey!

References

LCBO Vintage Chart 2006

World Wine Vintages Tables, Anthony Hawkins
August 1 2006

Wine Spectator Vintage Chart online. www.wine-spectator.com/wine/vintage/_charts_grid

Lee M. Cunningham is the proud owner of

Fore Vintages
Bobcaygeon, Canada
www.forevintages.com

About Fore Vintages
At Fore Vintages we offer a unique way of incorporating all, or part of wine, food, golf and travel into a fun, memorable learning experience. Whether it is a wine tasting or a wine tasting with food pairing after a day of golf, Fore Vintages can make it happen for you.

We have extensive knowledge and experience in all areas. We pride ourselves in teaching this in a simple yet informative manner.

We can be reached via email at **info@forevintages.com,** and be sure to check out our web site at **www.ForeVintages.com**. We will help you with your next memorable experience.

The "How to" Series of Books

This "How to" series of books was created to make those special things we like to enjoy in life less intimidating and easier to understand. Our goal is to get you the information you need to know in order to make a good decision. We give you the basic knowledge you need to be better informed, saving you endless amounts of time researching. We have done the hard work for you, condensed it down and put it in an easy to read format.

Good luck and enjoy.

About the Author

Lee M. Cunningham first became a golf professional in 1989. Throughout his career working at different clubs he always showed an interest in food. Trading off with different Chefs, Lee received cooking lessons in exchange for golf lessons. He then discovered that he had a passion for wine as well. An avid collector for the past 18 years, Lee has continually furthered his education about wine and the industry.

An avid traveler and self taught person, he has always enjoyed sharing his experiences with people to help them become more educated about wine, food, and golf. That's where the concept of the "How to" series of books came from.

Lee has now combined his passion for golf, food, wine and travel into a new business. His company **Fore Vintages** combines all of these elements to educate people in a way that they can easily grasp the concepts. Whether he is teaching golf, organizing golf excursions, or holding wine or food tastings, he enjoys sharing his passions with the public.